WHAT DO SPORTS ATHLETES EAT?

SPORTS BOOKS

Children's Sports & Outdoors Books

BABY PROFESSOR

EDUCATION KIDS

Speedy Publishing LLC
40 E. Main St. #1156
Newark, DE 19711
www.speedypublishing.com

You need equipment to play sports, correct? Would you even think about playing baseball without a bat? Soccer without shin guards? The answer to these questions would be no. To play sports you need the most important equipment – your body being fueled completely and ready to go! Unfortunately, many kids play sports without the nutrition their bodies need. We must eat healthy before any activity.

Read further to learn what the athletes eat and how you can eat healthy to fuel your body for the sports you love.

Green breakfast smoothie in bowl with superfoods on top.

WHEN TO EAT

It's all about the timing. If you eat too much, even if it is healthy, you may be sluggish and end up having an upset stomach or a stomach cramp. If you don't eat anything prior to exercising you may feel tired, faint or weak. To best prepare yourself for the day it is a good idea to eat a breakfast that is healthy.

If you know that you are going to eat a big meal, consume it three to four hours before you begin exercising. If you do eat closer to your activity, eat only a healthy, smaller meal. You will also need to eat after your activity in order for your muscles to recover.

Healthy food.

Healthy fruit and vegetable nutrition for kids.

WHAT SHOULD I EAT?

The main source of energy for your body is carbohydrates, so you will want to eat foods that are healthy, low in fat, and high in carbohydrates. Your body uses the carbs for energy. Some good carb choices are breads, vegetables, cereals, rice, fruit, and pasta. Fats and proteins are best to eat after exercise to replenish your muscles. Meat, nuts, and dairy products are great examples.

It is also important to keep hydrated, and the best source is water. If you are going to be exercising for more than 60 minutes, a sports drink such as Gatorade is a good source of hydration. The American College of Sports Medicine recommends that you follow the chart below to keep hydrated and stay healthy while exercising:

- Drink enough liquid to balance your daily liquid losses. On the days where the humidity and temperature are high, you will likely need more.

- Drink about 2 to 3 cups (0.5 to 0.8 liters) of water prior to your exercise.

- Drink about 2 to 3 cups (0.5 to 0.8 liters) of water after you exercise for each pound (0.5 kilogram) of weight you lose during your workout.

- Drink roughly 1 cup (0.25 liters) of water every 15 to 20 minutes while you are exercising. You may need more if you have a larger body or the temperature is warmer.

Each person is different and you need to listen to your body to guide you as to what to eat and when to eat. Learn what is best for you. You might want to keep a journal for a couple of days to see what you are eating and how much you are eating to ensure that you are getting all the nutrients your body needs.

Greek yogurt in a glass jars.

IRON AND CALCIUM

Iron and calcium are to very important nutrients that every kid needs, even if they are not exercising. Iron provides the body with energy and calcium helps to build strong bones.

  Calcium can be found in dairy products such as milk, cheese, and yogurt. Some additional sources are dark green, leafy vegetables and products that are calcium fortified such as orange juice.

Iron can be consumed by eating foods such as dried beans, meat, and fortified cereals. Keep in mind that if your body does not receive enough iron you may get tired easily.

Various leafy vegetables.

Cat and mouse healthy lunch, fun food art for kids.

SHOULD I DIET?

The answer to that is a great big NO! As a kid athlete, your body has to have every possible opportunity to reach the size it is intended. If a teammate or coach makes a suggestion that you should alter your diet to take off or put on weight, be sure to check with your parents or other adult that you trust. You will also want to avoid any diet aids or supplements as they may damage your growing body. Eating healthy is a good idea at any age. As a child athlete, you are busy and may have a difficult time finding time for eating healthy.

Discuss this with your parents to see if they can come up with suggestions. It is a better idea to have a cooler in the car that has fresh fruit, a sandwich, and water than to drive through a fast food restaurant. Planning ahead is well worth it!

Remember that the number 1 piece of equipment is your body. If you take care of it and eat healthy, you will perform at your best and feel your best. Eat healthy!

Selection of complex carbohydrates.

WHAT ARE CARBOHYDRATES (CARBS)?

Alot of people are referring to starchy foods such as rice, bread, or pasta, or sugary foods like cake, candy, and cookies when they are talking about carbohydrates. Scientists are referring to specific kinds of molecules when they are talking about carbs.

Carbs are included in the four major organic molecule groups; the other three are Lipids (Fats), Nucleic Acids (DNA) and Proteins. Carbohydrates consist of three separate elements: Oxygen, Hydrogen and Carbon.

WHAT DO CARBS DO?

They are vital to daily lives of all living organisms. Carbs provide necessary energy for cells with glucose, they store energy using starches, and provide structure for living plants and many animals.

TYPES

Carbohydrates are often referred to as saccharides. Each type has the word *"Saccharide"* as part of the name.

Sugar.

MONOSACCHARIDES - Monosaccharides are the most basic form and includes sugars like fructose and glucose. Often, they will dissolve in water and taste sweet. Glucose is the common carb found in plants and it is the main product of the photosynthesis process.

DISACCHARIDES - Disaccharides are formed using two Monosaccharides. They are also referred to as sugars such as lactose and sucrose. Milk contains this carbohydrate.

OLIGOSACCHARIDES - Oligosaccharides form from a small number of monosaccharides, usually three to six.

POLYSACCHARIDES - Polysaccharides consist of long carbohydrate molecules and are also known as complex carbohydrates.

Goji berries, a form of polysaccharide.

COMPLEX CARBOHYDRATES

Complex Carbohydrates are categorized in four different types:

STARCHES are how many plants retain energy. We then consume the starches and our bodies utilizes the energy.

GLYCOGEN is needed by animals to store energy. It is stored in our liver and muscles for use when needed.

CELLULOSE is utilized in plants as a structural molecule. It cannot be processed by animals.

CHITIN is utilized as a structural molecule in arthropods and fungi.

WHAT HAPPENS TO ANY CARBOHYDRATES THAT ARE LEFT OVER?

When we consume carbs, our body utilizes them as energy. If we consume more than our body can use, it coverts them to fat, which is used as energy for later. Our bodies try to keep energy for later when we haven't consumed any carbs.

Raw sweet potatoes.

LIPIDS

Lipids are another part of the four organic molecule groups and consist of the same elements as carbs do; oxygen, hydrogen and carbon. However, they usually have several more hydrogen atoms than they have oxygen atoms.

Waxes, phospholipids, steroids, and fats are all lipids. One distinct characteristic is that they will not dissolve in water.

Lipids play a vital role with living organisms, with some of their functions including cell membranes, hormones, and energy storage.

FATS

Fats are made of a glycerol molecule and three fatty acid molecules. As in all lipids, fats consist of carbon, oxygen and hydrogen molecules. It is used by our bodies as energy storage.

Not all fats are bad. They are actually needed for our bodies to remain healthy and we could not live without our diets consisting of some fats.

Fish oil capsules next to sprat.

Typically, people will need to consume about 20% to 30% of their diet from fats, but, too much fat is not good for your body to remain healthy. Too much of it can cause you to be to heavy and may clog your arteries.

Fats are divided into two major categories: *Saturated Fats* and *Unsaturated Fats.*

SATURATED FATS remain solid when at room temperature. They tend to come from foods such as red meat, butter, and cheese. They are often referred to as *"Bad"* fats since they can result in high cholesterol, clog our arteries, and possibly increase the risk for certain cancers.

UNSATURATED FATS become liquid when at room temperature. They typically come from certain foods such as fish, vegetables and nuts. They are much healthier for you than saturated fats are and are often referred to as *"Good"* fats.

Selection of healthy fat sources.

WAXES

Waxes are comparable to fats with their chemical make up, but they have only one long, fatty acid chain. They are soft when at room temperatures. Waxes are produced by plants and animals typically are used for protection. Plants utilize waxes to help retain water. We have wax in our ears which helps to protect our eardrums.

Red apple.

STEROIDS

Any group of lipids are steroids. They include hormones, chlorophyll and cholesterol. Our bodies need cholesterol to make the male hormone testosterone and the female hormone estrogen. Plants use chlorophyll for absorption of light need for photosynthesis.

You may have heard that steroids are bad for you. As you read, not all of them are bad. We need steroids like cortisol and cholesterol to survive. Steroids can also be used for people that are sick.

However, the steroids that you hear and read about in sports, known as anabolic steroids, can be really bad for your body. They can cause severe damage to your body such as liver damage, blood clots, kidney failure and strokes.

PHOSPHOLIPIDS

This is the fourth major group of lipids. Phospholipids have a very similar chemical make up to fats. They are one of the key structural elements of all cell membranes.

Now that you have learned about eating healthy, are you ready to go play some sports? Exercise and healthy eating work hand in hand to keep your body healthy as you grow.

For additional information, you can go to your local library, research the internet, and ask questions of your teachers, family and friends.

Visit
BABY PROFESSOR
EDUCATION KIDS
www.BabyProfessorBooks.com
to download Free Baby Professor eBooks
and view our catalog of new and exciting
Children's Books